THE PRIMROSE PATH

MARTY PASCO

◆ FriesenPress

Suite 300 - 990 Fort St
Victoria, BC, V8V 3K2
Canada

www.friesenpress.com

Copyright © 2020 by Marty Pasco
First Edition — 2020

Illustrations by Keelan Horne

All rights reserved.

No part of this publication may be reproduced in any form, or by any means, electronic or mechanical, including photocopying, recording, or any information browsing, storage, or retrieval system, without permission in writing from FriesenPress.

ISBN
978-1-5255-6045-3 (Hardcover)
978-1-5255-6046-0 (Paperback)
978-1-5255-6047-7 (eBook)

1. POETRY, SUBJECTS & THEMES, DEATH, GRIEF, LOSS

Distributed to the trade by The Ingram Book Company

Primrose Path—*a life led by ease and pleasure, often ending in calamity.*

Very unsure of what the end of this phase will reveal, but I am hopeful. I will say the path is an intriguing one and this is my story of what I have followed thus far. Almost all of these poems were written between the spring of '18 and the spring of '19. Most poems have been written in the way that I would speak them because I do believe this collection is better off heard, than read. Regardless, I have put them together for very simple reasons: the inspiration from friends to do so and because I am sick of carrying around three journals and risking the chance of losing it all. It would also be a blessing to "profit" from writing down my feelings, in whatever form "profit" takes. I hope readers can relate and/or have a laugh and a cry while flipping through these pages. I will admit that some of these poems are very contradictory to this book being in print, but Gord said it best: *"We live to survive our paradoxes."*

Thanks.

Enjoy!

Table of Contents

DECADENCE 3

Just Like These Streets 5
Newschool Old-Schooler 8
Twenty-Six Letters? 9
Whose Bum? 11
Hand to Mouth 12
What is Mine? 13
Where and When 14
The Wind is My Only Friend 14
Just to Say Something 15
Ashes and Ashes 16
Holy Moly 18
God Dog Day 20
The Concoction 22
The Problem 24
My Scare-people 25
expression and Impression 27
Drink Ol' Boy? 28
"Coping" 30
Primrose Path 33

BABE IN THE WOODS 39

A New Light 41
Naked as We Came 42
Her Fireside 43

- Onions and Eggs 44
- Passenger-Seat Pleasures 46
- Let it be Tonight 47
- You and the Bee 49
- Safe Ground 50
- Hide and Don't Seek 51
- Five and a Half Years 52
- Stand Together 53
- Huckleberry Girl 54
- Galena Baby 54
- **Ash, Cash, or Run** 55
- Full-Time Loving 56

PLEASE STAND BY 59

- Within the Ribs 60
- The Four of Us 61
- Dreams Away 62
- Shine Your Guns 63
- No One Needs to Know! 64
- The First Sight Of William Wallace 66
- Sandpaper My Soul 67
- STUNT 68
- Ease Your Mind, My Sister 69
- The Storytellers 70
- Blood 72
- I Can't Call It 74
- This One's for Them 77
- Old Friend 79

The Ballad of Johnny Peterson 83

Poets aren't brilliant!

If poets were brilliant then what would you call Einstein?

A poet?

Sure enough,

> "Name: Albert Einstein
>
> Occupation: Poet"

There you go, brilliance.

How smart it was to take this short line about poets being average to . . .

voilà,

there once was a brilliant poet.

A news piece.

Brilliant.

Just Like These Streets

A countryside ride, with gravel road delights.
No rules till we hit highway pavement lights.
Acquainted by an assortment of joyriders and bottles alike.
Competing all of a sudden with the heavy flowing veins of night.
Driving southbound transfixed,
the most hypnotized of wildlife
The ones tearing for a wild night,
> they were.

When a pair danced down bus stairs,
> staggering in love and in hug
>> on the six cities and their streets I don't know.

I must have stumbled into coke-binged moods,
frantic, hustling words
from the tongues of the dancing lovers.
> One used to be mine.
> But now she plays mother
> and I call her out on fluttering jib jab
> behind cigarettes.

Bus-stop leaner-uppers,
street curb lurkers
with quick-flirt worders
perking up for a wrestle
while the rest mark awkward silence with sips of stiff drinks
> inside the restaurant.

We treat it more like a bar
> as we shit shoot at the odd listening ear.

Some words blow minds like a dish drop.
> Stealing attention.

The trend-head at the end of the table dabbles in his hair and rings,
> piercings, and rolled-up jeans.
> Socks match for sure.

While the sock-less, shoeless pretty boy catches his old blonde babe back with yet another tale about crossing through the thundering prairies.
> Thumbing patiently during Canada's first taste of rain,
> still mainly snow.

Not blaming the blonde babe.
> His glow could hold the room.
> His small talk could shatter your dreams
> along with your night of caring for anyone else.

Just like these streets,
that don't try to hide their beauty and bad behaviour.
So while the night is young,
we cross the city with tainted tongues.
> We roam between high-rises to feel we belong,
> and find the dirt that lies within,
> the ass of Ontario,
> the home of friend and kin.

They don't have to impress me.
> So I let myself in.

What does impress me is the dwindling of whiskey and the empty beer bottles on the drowning table.

As the night begins to turn
from casual to electric,
we are ready to be heard
the flavour is infectious.
The upstairs neighbour, however,

made sure to sternly word his disapproval of our decadent debauchery.

> "Kick the door in my friend,
> You'll find nudity and coitus,
> A flower shower of we don't give no hoots to brute fools of the sleepy night!"

We live on the cheap;
the too cheap to the point it's probably not good for us.
We squander paycheques and mama's lending hand.
The founders of ecstasy,
the heroines of being beat,
keeping par with the poets and the beat keepers in the streets
with the broken bums; we weep
with the tourists of a Friday's moon; we scream.
And just like these streets,
that don't try to hide their foul and intangible whispers,
we are not dressed in yesterday's disguise.
We puke our voices into our hands and drop them from roof tops,

>just to see which ones survive.

We know better than to mind the eyes,

>being witnessed is past the point.

We have been told to get with the times,
and so we have chosen to live naked,

>as the streets at night.

So let us be heard as insane,
let us burn down the homes of being sound,
let us question everything before us
and blow it all to pieces.
If we so wish.

Newschool Old-Schooler

I'm sick of getting my kicks out of someone else's story.
I'm sick of getting my kicks out of someone else's life.
I'm sick of getting my kicks out of bullshit said on the street.
I'm sick of getting my kicks from memories of old.
I'm sick of getting my kicks from the "promising" future.
I'm sick of getting my kicks from dreams never lived.
I'm sick of trying to kick these habits.

So I'll take this kick and freak the funk out!
I'll cock this kick and absorb the aftershock.
I'll take this kick and a grow a million eyes.
I'll take this kick and squeeze out everything it has,
        suck dry every vessel, morsel, valve and vein,
        chew on it for taste.
I'll run with these kicks and blame the moon,
for these good times are birthed from the night.
These kicks are hexed and frightening.
But I'm primed like lightning in a bottle.
So let's release these kicks for the kick of it,
        chase what reverberates,
        seize the beat,
        and keep on kickin' it!

Twenty-Six Letters?

My words are lonely lately.
Lost in the thoughts of my lady, maybe.
Slipping through my fingertips.
Staining steering wheel, safely
    engraving
    pavement
with tire-tread scriptures.
Outlining pictures of angels with poetry, hopefully.
Oh, my words are lonely lately.

Lost in the thoughts of my baby's ex babies, maybe.
Unsafely engraving my memory box,
a tough topic,
Lock it, toss it.
Oh, my words are lonely lately.
Wading and waiting,
way out,
slowly swimming seaward.
They are sea words now, searching for an insightful use,
lost and lonely.
Oh, my words are lost and lonely lately,
and I can't blame them.
Not satisfying my craving for intellectual safety,
they're naked,
or dressed in a tuxedo-tied knot, I suppose you would say.
A simple grey,
no shimmer or shine of violet,
just a simple grey.

Oh, my simple words are lost and lonely lately.

Twenty-six letters floating on a feather
waiting to be collected.
But they are nowhere near.
A long, long way from here.
So I drive and drive and drive and drive,
with my journal on the dashboard,
my legs crossed,
my eyes following birds in the rearview,
my mind eyeing the feather that flutters from it,
my imagination forming fragments in the trees
that might lead me
to that lonely, lonely, lonely,
simple lost and lonely place
my words have been lately.

Whose Bum?

Look at the bum in the park nursing a cigarette and a hangover.
Look at how his eyes slowly close as his pockets get robbed by
the pinecones.
A stone's throw away is his home because it is where his pack lays.
He probably just masturbated in the sushi restaurant down the street
because all his friends left him lonely years ago.
He's definitely not married because he sits alone.
Wow, he has a phone,
For masturbation purposes only, I presume.

My ice cream melts in my bowl as he wipes the sweat from his brow.
I can see it in his eyes—he is still fighting sleep and the thought of
buying another six-pack to get him through the desert day and ice
cream cold night that are upon us,
Slowly growing,
like his chances of getting cancer as he outs his cigarette.

I finish my ice cream as his eyelids melt and finally close,
I walk away
and pick up a pine cone from the driveway.

Hand to Mouth

From hand to mouth I was fed,
only needing to breathe on the tit.
Hand to mouth I was led,
only needing to heave the lips.
Hand to mouth the money death paid thee to lighten thy shoulder.
Hand to mouth and I'm out of jail bar duties, thanks to death.
So, hand to mouth, I ripped through grocery store dumpsters,
I reaped what was free and lived so cheaply,
so cheaply,
in order to pay my respects for saving my weak
ass.
Hands and mouth to myself now.
Hand to mouth, blow a kiss in thanks.
Hand to mouth and I'm out,
back on the road in a blink,
the only place to go ... when you really need a
job.
And hand to mouth I will sip now,
and sip, and sip, and sip, hoping for relief in the persistence of
hand to mouth.
But for now, from hand to mouth, I will live
within the drain and drag
of abusing
my hands
and my mouth.

What is Mine?

Oh it's been raining lately, baby.
Flooding this jail-cell mind of mine
And all I had was laid out on the line
And, oh,
Did that rain come down!
Blew everything I owned all over town.
And off I went with my head hung.
Stumbling, soaking wet,
it cut me down a size,
stretched my last sweater, one more time.
Hopeless, but not helpless yet.

"Have you seen any getaway britches around by chance, sir?
All my belongings have been thrown about."

> "Young man, come on in,
> get out of the rain, sit down.

Let me tell you something about the lost and found."

Where and When

Fog horn blows, hey, ho.
We're home, where we will die
and still worry about it.
Where we'll practice living
till it's time to give up.
Where will we hide!?
Where will we waste our time?
How will we spend it?
What a life.
Constantly dying, get high to see if it won't happen.
Entrapment,
with no constant to revert to.
Mom, I'm scared
Will I make it?
Or cry my way back to you?
Mother, my helper,
are you home?

The Wind is My Only Friend

The wind is my only friend.
She kisses me good morning.
Holds me at day's end.
She tells me her stories
of the places she's been.
The wind is my only friend.

Just to Say Something

Smoke quiet child while the sun is out.
The landlord agrees with me.
I don't speak much else other than,
    "I'm going for a cigarette."
But after a drink I can talk.
It breaks the restraint that is my father and releases my mother's tongue
It never comes out knowledgeable but it doesn't have to, to fit in
with the normality of others.
But "it's not poetic," my father would say
Coming from a fashionista doesn't mean much to me anyway.
Let me just smoke and sit with not even my thoughts being heard.
I'm not much of a talker anyhow.
But a drink may be good.

Ashes and Ashes

Come grab my heart.
      Tear it apart
before this next set
      of cigarettes.
Come humble me
      like a tumbled leaf
Before this next set
      of cigarettes.
Come open my eyes
      before I burn
this last set
      of cigarettes.

Come take my home
      from long ago.
Shake the cave
      and my feet below.
Rage the pavement
      where flowers grow.
Make the sex.
      But leave me the rest.
      With this last set
      of cigarettes.

Don't wait for me.
Just waste on me.
It's the waste I need to grieve in,

> over the never-ending fairytale,
> which is yet to be told.
> Yet to be honed in,
> just a distant dim light
> beyond the smoke.

The beginning is near.
If I could only afford it,
kick habits and go for it,

> I'm just not quite sold on the whole of it.

But I'm getting mighty sick of having nothing—
potential, but nothing

> Daring and faring out
> with nothing.

If I just had something
> to leave behind
this wandering through
of this next set
> of cigarettes.

Well, I could bet
that if I burned and turned
> over enough times
my life would still fulfill
> to yet another pile of ashes.
Burning next
to my last set
> of cigarettes.

Holy Moly

I'm holy everywhere.
    Like, holy moly.
My girl, my world so bright and pink.
How could I have done this to myself, my girl?
I wonder, my honey,
why a breeze blows the trees over?
Like I wonder how I blew us off the oh so lovely, windy, honey-moon map?
    Blasphemy!
    My holy jeans,
        my frozen toes due to wear,
        my empty accounts
            due to not caring,
            worth a fuck.
A devious past
led to a deceitful path.
Not a girl or the world's fault
I wore these holes,
set them, as stones in my soul,
and broke the tools to fix them.
Any accounts I could bank on are empty and sinking.
    Roped up,
    toes up,
    and running from the ways my father told me to grow up!
Holy moly!
What a dope stuck, crawling
    through the mud,
    through the muddy path I then again rained on.

It was a path I wasn't really using anyway.
> Too lazy to make a footstep.
> Too bothered by the way the last one looked
And, oh, did I place it there,
sunk in with my heavy head and crooked crown,
stuck on one leg now,
like the next one might not appear at all.
> Limbo-o-o-oooo! Fall!
But hold on now.
> While you're bent and meant to fall,
> reach down, unlace the holy soled boot
> that has concreted you to the past
> and bank on your last holy thread
> you call your one and only heart string.
Reach out that bare foot.
Prepare for the ride as you slide over cotton-candy fields and dew-flossed grass.
Spring has finally set
for your holy moly,
singing heart.

GOD DOG DAY

Everyone is fucked up in one way or another.

You either have a vice or a device and I'm not sure which one is better.

OK, maybe we're not all fucked up—

just a little crooked.

OK, maybe not right now, but we will be.

OK, turn around and take a little look-see.

> If there is nothing there, well, swallow your tongue and hold onto your nightmares 'cause you need that shit to remind you you're still alive.
>
> Because sometimes all ya got is a full ashtray to remind you that everything ya got will burn away someday.

So smoke 'em if ya got 'em and I don't just mean cigarettes.

Love what ya got while ya got it,

> people while they're here.

'Cause everyone has a different way to the bottom

or the sky, however you wanna see it.

The only real guarantee is:

> Every dog dies one day, so,
>
> what are your wishes for tomorrow?
>
> Every dog dies one day, so,
>
> what are your wishes for today?

I know it seems like such a long, long way away, but every dog dies one day, so,

> what do you wish you did instead?
>
> What do you wish you did yesterday?

And you can't blame the druggies and alcoholics.

It's a heavy burden to barter with.

A beast of burden, some call it.

That damn beast on the wall that counts to twelve.
That damn face that *should* scream:
> *"Now is the hour with the power;*
> *tomorrow will fall."*

But sounds more like your mother asking you to:
> *"Clean your bedroom*
> *and sweep the hall."*

And at that point, I guess it's all time's fault for not saying,
> *"Wake the fuck up, kid!"*

But time won't die.
The only face that lives forever.
And I'd bet it's safe to say that if time was a dog, with a day to die,
he'd be howling with the wolves, fighting it off like a dirty cough that won't go away!
And on that note,
are you just going to take another day off to be fucked up
or are you gonna find time and grab it by the balls and say,
> *"Let's go!"*

There's no shame in the blame game but time is just a face securely fastened to your wall.
So you gonna let time keep you fucked up,
> twisted, listed, crooked, and ass-kissing,

or you gonna use being fucked up to turn yourself around and continue to reap,
every god dog day?

The Concoction

I need to find something that gets me growing more than liquor, love, cigarettes, writing, hard work and adrenaline sports.
Maybe something like running up and down stairs for hours on end, or yoga.
Maybe something like masturbation or junk
but something less scary,
like travelling.
But something more along the lines of making my parents proud.
Like Jesus.
But not like Jesus.
Maybe like meditation,
but something more demanding.
Something that will make me fly,
like sex,
but a little less demanding.
Like sleep,
but more productive.
Maybe doing something that's good for me will be good for me right now. . . .
Like brushing my teeth!
But more something I actually want to do,
like staring at the stars
I love staring at the stars, and it can't be bad for me.
But something a little more fulfilling would be great.
Something that satisfies like a buffet.
Something that leaves me crying in bliss,
With nothing lost,

and anything gained.

Maybe whiskwah is the answer!

Maybe whiskwah is the answer!

Maybe I'll just continue drinking whiskey water wishing I believed in a god so I could fly higher and scare the shit out of myself and have it be pleasurable.

That's exactly it!

I'll drink whiskey with water while I puff cigarettes and have sex with a goddess that I love while skydiving with my eyes closed thinking about nothingness in lotus position and with my free hand I'll write a free-verse poem about it all.

The concoction.

The Problem

He had a drinking problem.
She had the answers for him.
She said let's drink together.
And together they cried,
through love-stained eyes.
For two years nothing was said.
For two years they stayed in bed.
For too long they painted that bed red
with fear
of being alone.
He had nothing to share.
She had wine and money.
And together they cried,
through wine-stained eyes.

My Scare-people

I was thrown for a loop when you told me you're scared of being alone.
I'm home, alone.
I'm not scared of the laughs or the tears people bring,
shared, or in close pairs.
But I fare out most of the time without receiving a fix from the rest of the nonsense.
So I built myself a scare-people.
To steer clear the peers of bullshit.
To mislead the leaders who think they know me
and to freak the keepers of structured belief from my door.
I'm not a homebody, not a somebody,
and I don't mind being a nobody to you,
so I'm sorry, but scoot.
It's brutal, but the loop is small
and most don't fit through,
thanks to my scare-people
who holds down the fort.

This scare-people wears no shoes,
he has a shirt that says
    "Fuck you!"
He's blunt, says cunt, and his hair is dirty.
He doesn't brush his teeth,
he smells like liquor and cigarettes,
a drunken punk thief that leaves you rude,
with no regrets of his own.
His soul is dark like unburnt coal folded over the pastel night that is his heart.

DECADENCE

His mind leaks battery acid over the holy moulds
His hands touch only the lonely hopes.
His eyes bleed a mask of smoke.
And he is the caretaker of the growing garden
that is my future
of being alone.

EXPRESSION AND IMPRESSION

i may start with: to each their own.

Proper, primed, and shined for appearance
seems like struggle to me.
"Feet off the coffee table, your coffee to."
What's a table for again?
Oh, yeah,
it just sits there looking pretty in a pretty room.
If looking pretty is what it's all about then i would lose over and over again.
my beard is growing in nicely though.
But my sleeves are sloppy and droop over the shrimp cocktail.
my words better be smart here,
but this ship is so divine it intrudes on my definition of proper.
i relate more to the dead shrimp that i suck and the turkey crisped in the pan
than i do to the gold around the dishes rim.
i relate more to the dogs laying under the table that await a stray bite
than i do with the Portuguese wine that is recommended for sipping.
Recommendations and reputations have never tickled
my not-so-fancies.
Appearances mean nothing anyway when you're wearing makeup.
Smart words are only smart if they aren't a disguise.
When everything is riddled with silver it helps to catch an eye
but why, must we feel we need to be seen?

Being a classy intellect is one thing;
me being a shithead is another.

Sorry.

Drink Ol' Boy?

If I had a bottle of whiskey would I still sit and sulk like I'm fucking
Steven Glansberg?
A dull dog, a drowned rat, sad.
Would I try to make a joke with another human being,
maybe try to impress on first impressions?
Aaeehh, that's ridiculous!
No one really cares, no one really matters
I don't really care, I don't really matter.
But if there was a bottle of whiskey, then ...

> "Aaha, that's like this one time I met Jesus in San Francisco.
> Turns out he loves his wine and he whines to preach drunk
> around 2 a.m. in motel rooms."

But without the whiskey ...

> my pen doesn't move.
> A lonely pen.

While I go to try and say hi
to the lonely men, and women too.

> "Hey, how are you, where ya from?
> Oh, Ontario. Me, too. Whereabouts?
> Oh, a small town. Me, too.
> Whoopidee fucking doo!"

Where's the whiskey or Jesus's wine?
Tell me the truth!
I don't care where from, or who is who.
Tell me about You.
Tell me about the You that can't be read,
the You that scares You to breathe through.

Let me watch You be scared while you scream obscenities of your own sorrows and joys!
Tell me the last time you cried,
the last time you made true love,
and how those intertwined.
Tell me the last time you got stabbed at a bar down in Florida and decided to kill the man.
Throw something at me,
make me cry,
make me love you,
make my knees cripple,
make me want to go back to Florida for old time's sake.
Or maybe not.
I'm banned from the states—long story, tell ya later.
But heeeeyy!
How about a shot of whiskey, old boy?

"COPING"

This one I'll write for my wrongs and the devil
while I'm up all night drinking at another level.
When I'm headful of problems and let go's.
I can't seem, to let go of the devil
> that says let's go,
>> just one more time for a walk down the street to the store that sells hope.

But the hope that I'm finding isn't binding the patches.
It just helps to cope with the mind games and to bury the hatches.
> For the night, at least.

When morning comes, just bury it in cigarette ashes, and dash quick to a stumble
into last night's leftovers—
a little stale but who cares.
It's like slapping the dog that bit me
but the hair of the dog just fits me
Until I'm back to sleep not twitching,
> sweating, and fretting;
> not itching
> to do anything.

This one I'll write for my wrongs and the devil.
For all the nights where all I did was revel.
But as of late, I have even beveled with that.
No party, no voice.
I just slide on through the cracks and on back to what I now lack as I smoke the last in the pack, alone, in drunken home where the walls cry and the sky dies a little, by my second-hand smoke.

At the same time, that hand lands for another slam from the scam that is,

    my "coping."

My mom doesn't know that I'm "coping."
My dad definitely doesn't know that I'm "coping."
But that's just cause I don't call anymore.

    And, fuck, she doesn't call anymore!

This fucking curveball that has occurred has got me face down in the dirt.
A drunken, fucking introvert, that only knows how to flirt with a bottle!
Surprise, surprise, Jim Morrison's my role model.
But too lazy to read a novel.
Too busy groveling over problems with no way to solve them.
It's so easy to succumb to the toxins when it seems you've run out of options.
Fuck it, I'm done.
No more proceeding with caution.
I've lost it!
Where is the gun?
Where is that little man? I'm done.
I'm sick of this wasteland.
This in-high-command, demanding devil in my hand.
I'm done!
No more hoping or coping.
Just run!
From the devil on my shoulder to...
the One!

DECADENCE

      To the one that doesn't call anymore.
      To the one with all the answers, all the cures.
      The one that has caused this mess
      and the one that can patch it.
      She didn't send the devil—
      I chose to unlatch him.
But without him.
And while beside her,
I can rest and fester
as she releases the pressure
with which I was,
"coping."

Primrose Path

The busy,
whimsical
freakshow.
Death
breeds
running.

Too much of a glorious thing.
Propagating
heroes on the wall.
The only way.
My grandfather's
Primrose Path.

Heinously high.
Airborne.
Fathom this:
bullets
need
impact.

Welcoming
negligence
to roam,
swallow
the tongue of
craving.

DECADENCE

Chasing
insufficient
hands.
Existence,
possibly only in
our reveries.

Falling forward forever
to miss the train to heaven.
Kissing the edge on the way by.
Not stopping, just joining the end of the line,
trying all over again for the first time.
Head down
the Primrose Path

Excuse.
Abuse.
It's the thing to do.
Don't slow.
Don't slow.
Don't cope.

Go.
Just go!
Sharks in the water.
Can't be forgotten.
Just a head above
the rotten.

Hurray!
Bombay
flames in the
loafing,
soaking
pleasure.

Forever,
the outlet,
upset
culprit,
hate others.
My lover.

Atheism
is bashful
so tiptoe
through halos
for a handful
of beans.

Throw down
the lowdown.
Corncob
pipe
and a button
for dessert.

DECADENCE

Pumpkin hippy
cake dripping
melting
relentlessly
to dissolve
till tomorrow.

Re-borrow
time
with a line.
Re-live.
No sand.
Just sandpaper.

Flattened,
tattered
with thanks.
Someday,
dry up.
No thanks.

Elope from boot liners.
Cry.
Broke
with loot miners.
Crawl
under the rug.

No, no
honey-suckle.
It's all locked away.
Ease
comes to play.
Here we go.

Eat
or be eaten,
in the end.
So suck the sugar apples
and sit
or be sat-in.

Embellish in forbidden fruit.
Drop
dead
on the road
of lustrous hope.
The Primrose Path.

Sniff sinful bliss
of herb
in limelight circles.
Yesterday's joke
promised
in the book.

DECADENCE

Today's mystery
locked
maybe took
relish regardless.
Time is near.
Presents here.

No mismanaged
last minutes.
Please wipe my ass.
Please, please, no.
De-rail me first.
The Primrose Path.

The Primrose Path.
Indulgence,
at the base.
Leisure
in the game.
Know,
no end.

Babe in the Woods

A New Light

I walked out my front door.
Had an orgasm this morning.
I felt the grass beneath my feet.
And again got a little horny.
Sunshine and rainbows.
Your mind and a halo.
What is this faceful
of this beautiful, tasteful mirage that has unfolded before me?
Where am I?
      good morning,
      magic morning,
flourishing in the spring that is growing
out my front door.

No more pouring of thorny roses or mornings of heavy doses.
No more hard-hitting psychosis.
I'm back to free-range coasting, a daily four courses
      of magic
awaits, out the front door.

Naked as We Came

I haven't touched your hips for too many months, my lady.
I've been hung high and wet by my savings account
and around here it rains acid, baby.
So go hide somewhere in the southern mountains and I'll come
find you,
you and the river.
It's been too long and I'm unsure of what I'll say but fresh water will
help that along
and tonight, I don't fear the cold or the reaper, so here I am,
naked as I came.
I don't have much but what I do, it's all yours,
if you'll just join me.

Her Fireside

Distracted, but still infatuated by her.
Distant and away, but the stones we laid around the flame still hold loves residual.
I stand back and respect her for staying cool while I burn, smoky eyed, needing to believe that our brilliant minds think alike.
The fire thrives and I'll never tire, now beside her, fireside.

> "We are alive," the fire cries.
> "We can't see without each other.
> We can't be the love recovered,
> from sticks and stones

without room to breathe,
and space between us."

Onions and Eggs

Let's pledge we all have money
From unwitnessed mountain honey.
North or south, slave and heave,
bumming or not, reluctantly.
Eating beans and Canmore's greed
Not cooking, but using our hands more.
We're now flourishing
fully, completely.
Spending cautiously
But still eating
onions and eggs.
Wedged between the dream and sex talk.
Flocking, walking, lovers of the cave,
behaving like lava laid off a waterfall's spout,
calling "Did you see that!?"
Casplat!
Go the wingnuts and the liquor bottle cap.
We are no chickens,
we're lovers,
fending for ourselves, with the chickens' help
while we horse around in horse masks,
eat borscht off the floor
where hacky sack lies.
A good day for hay and mushrooms by the ocean.
While time it loans us
for our joy
and the comfort of "of course,

let's do it!"
Fruitless kaboomers of looming about,
rooming four to a double bed
Heading northwest—
quest-less, restless, and festering in a question-less fury,
in a hurry to say "fuck it, I'll eat it!"
Endless pits of shit, of course,
till our minds fell 10,000 feet to the ground
where safety was found,
along with the simple delights,
shining bright once more.
Like onions and eggs
in a dirty pan.

Passenger-Seat Pleasures

The jingling, jangling yellow crystal dances with the running boards.
The feather in the mirror zig zags and zooms over mountain passes,
reaching over and over to knock at the window.
Oh, the passenger-seat pleasures.
The back door gurgles and giggles as if being wiggled and tickled
by potholes—
troublesome,
tragic,
and trendy on Canada's highways.
The flamingo and the dinosaur fittle and flirt,
touching tips amongst coffee spills
and, ooooh, on big hills, ya just relax
'cause the seatbelt is wrapped up around the back too many times to be safe.
Just put your feet up and gaze, at the birds in the rain,
paying close attention to any new sounds from the engine
keep the driver high and hydrated,
fed and sometimes intoxicated,
the only duties within,
       passenger-seat pleasures.
Brainstorm a blanket fort
with the sexually frustrated of sorts
and never abort the crooked missionary,
no matter how quiet you must be.
The front-seat man understands
that every second asks for pleasure,
especially when the wheels are turning.

Let it be Tonight

So how about tonight you open up your lungs and sing me that song you're not sure how to sing but you play along most of the time because you know what it brings me.
So how about you let go of your tongue tonight and let fly every worry and dream you've ever held from me?
> 'Cause the light can't last forever and when the sun goes down so do the drinks and I can't wait that long cause I might not remember to bug you in that fleeting moment that can never last forever.

So how about tonight you open your eyes and see how dark it really is in this lonely home of flesh and bones?
So how about tonight you open your mouth and let your vocal cords be the gasoline, the kerosene that lifts your heavy words from your heavy heart?
> 'Cause if not the light might die and the drinks might cry heavier than ever before and I can't let that happen because I swore on us that it wouldn't.

So if tonight we can't blow your mind wide open, well, that's no option. Tonight we are going to blow your mind wide open and just wait to see what happens.

I'll melt with heavy shoulders if tomorrow it pours and all we do is sit and watch the puddles form, 'cause what happens will happen and I just happen to want to dance with you.
> So never mind a song, let's just scream and believe for a single second that no one can hear us.

> A single second of tonight is all that I am asking you for and from then on forth, our course will no longer be setting, but rising to the north.

So how about tonight, we shave down any feelings of remorse and divorce ourselves from judgement?

Let's live naked in more important ways.

Let's trade thoughts of passions like we do orgasms,

Hijack the outcomes and ride as long as we can with rigid and ripped rags for sails.

No, this love isn't perfection and neither is the boat but you are the one that made me tired of floating and I know you're ready to tell me where you want to go.

So tonight,

let me rip you open.

Let your blood run thin and don't be scared like you know I was.

Don't just go with the motions.

Let go of the emotions and let your heart cry, lying wide open.

So how about tonight

we scream things we have never said,

demand things we need instead of waiting for them to be,

do things never been done to turn our futures into lives we never thought we would live.

So tonight,

tell me how you really feel,

let this be the answer,

when you expect me

to do the same.

You and the Bee

When I die, bury me
deep below, with the honey bee.
Deep below the maple tree, please.
Leave me there, with my heart wide open,
wearing nothing but
> you.

Wrap my hand around a bottle,
> glue my lips to it,

tape my foot around the throttle,
> and let me rip, deep to the pit of
>> you.

And if you say no to being my clothes,
well, promise me, you and the bee
will carry on like two fairies,
my obituary,
> which simply reads,

>> "He lays, as he lived,
>> naked and drunk,
>> With his chest ripped wide open."

Safe Ground

you are the bird's song in the rain
lust ripping through a vein
the quiet during the war
the "welcome" at the door
the spur in the moment of it all
the white rain in the fall

Hide and Don't Seek

Let's get away, maybe stay away.
At least a hiding place for now
If you could lay me down,
put my drink on down
And sing to me as the rain falls down
in this non-existent town, well,

> I'd do it all for you,
> anything you ask.
> Everything more and nothing less
> as we rest away in the loneliness
> of a comfy cabin,
> caressed
> by each other.

No dire needs, only the fire pleads for more.
No one to please, no internet disease.
No knocking at the door.
No bad moods or forbidden fruits around.
No fast foods, no work boot attitudes.
No more sink, sand grounds.
All our troubles out the window.
Hustle bustle with the breeze blow.
And as for you and me,
we'll stay eloped,
'Cause within simplicity
there is forever hope.

Five and a Half Years

Well, I can't say for sure,
but if this letter reaches your door
I can't promise you'll love me anymore.
But this must be said.

Yesterday I sat on my front porch
adding up all that I adore
and not that money makes much sense
but this nickel and this half cent
are saying way more than ever before.
So to settle the score, I do some math.
Twenty minus twenty-five-and-a-half.
       Never mind the liquor.
       Never mind the gas
that leaves me sittin' on one poor ass.
With not a penny to shine,
buried under the line.
One broke boy at war with time.
At war with the age and yours without mine.
So never mind what makes cents.
Let your newfound youth be fare.
Let my reports on love bury the difference
and let us sit, broke with hope,
even
at zero.

Stand Together

A kiss for a kiss?
Or five for one?
An eye for an eye?
Or should we look in the same direction
instead
of heading at each other like cats?
A life for a life,
or shall we not follow
for there is crime in being superior.
Interfering will be forgiven,
vain thoughts on love will not.
I will leave,
if you take care.
Please stay when I stand up.
Please leave when I'm stale and staring.
Don't fall when I stand up.
Stand beside me,
let it be us,
in the fall.

Huckleberry Girl

She's a huckleberry girl
in her huckleberry world.
No diamonds and pearls.
Just long brown curls.
> She aims for high places
> where there are few faces.
> She fancies the fruit.
> Lunch, dinner, dessert.

Her knowledge is rooted
with the sweetness to prove it
in berry bushes' bloom.
> She's lost over the hills,
> far from the parties and thrills,

and she's found
at the very peak.

Galena Baby

Oh, mighty mountain
Oh, you mighty range.
I kneel at the foot of my bed for you.

ASH, CASH, OR RUN

The stars don't seem so distant tonight.
Actually, I think I just slipped on star dust.
But that could also have to do with my
cleanliness.
And that could be ash
from the ecstasy that I'm burning
and the shadow that's growing.
Ash or star dust floating, either way,
I'm chasin' it.
Running like the savage within.
Dead set on being rogue and dirty
while trying to capture what is feared.

Fame and lullaby nonsense.
Mix and wash each other in my
       clueless imagination.
        And the night falls on my head.

The stars don't seem so distant tonight.

Full-Time Loving

Let's quit our jobs, fall full time in love.
No big man, no boss or loss at all.
No greedy hands involved.
We'll pave our way to self-reliance with every drip of boiling blood we squeeze from our hearts.
I'll feed you if you wait for me to drink.
I'll give you my hand if you wait for me to leap.
I'll kiss you mist in the midst of the blistering heat.
Just wish me no more black-cloud afternoons.

I'll slave my hand to the bone to get you home.
Build bridges and boats to cross you to safety.
We'll make waves as we fall into full-time love.
So how about it,
we quit our jobs, fall full time in love?
In the spring we will work the field of what could be,
plant what we know beside what we don't.
With faith it will all grow into what we need.
We'll regrow our torn flesh on flowers.
Our gypsy ways will cling to the vines and veins, naturally
Our dream career will form from the days we don't waste craving dimes
The seeds of sex we blessed when we were lost will feed us tomorrow
if we need not worry.

In the fall we'll be humbled with the naked trees of the cold and poor
but natural kisses of poetry will weave us warmth.
The fountain of youth will re-magnetize our desires,
and consciousness, of all of this

will create every luxury you've ever missed.
No more "here we aren'ts."
No more "I wish I was there's."
No more being misled.
I promise you I won't.
And all we have to do is
quit our jobs and let this full-time love fall
right into place.

Please Stand By

WITHIN THE RIBS

I cried to you for the first time,
I let the scroll of my childhood completely unravel in front of you
and now your part of the script—
the cover, which I call: "Recognition from my father"—
has been lifted tonight, in front of you.
You split the ribs that kept his name from my whimpering heart
and I cried my weakened words of a real man to you,
for the first time.
Then again, if I was a real man, and him too,
we'd probably just shake hands and let the record play old sappy blues
tunes, and drink it all away,
as should be the tradition.
No one in the family knows how to shake hands anymore.
Or drink, for that matter.

The Four of Us

I thank them both for the liquor.
My father for his sternness that I don't miss,
my mother for the bickering that I have overcome,
and myself for being born.

My father for a few golden words,
my mother for the rain drops on my tongue,
and myself for using this all wisely.

My father for leaving me alone,
my mother for welcoming me home,
and myself for noticing that.

My father for his persistent nature,
my mother for her acceptance of my failures,
and myself for adapting.

My father for these calloused hands,
my mother for picking the rocks from them,
and myself for falling down.
And I thank Hope, for getting me back up.

I wouldn't want to let any of them see me being a dope stuck in the mud,
even though most days I'm just a pig in shit,
grinnin',
just to be smitten to it all.
And I hope Hope understands that, 'cause
my parents want me to be somebody.

Dreams Away

Dreams don't write books,
they create the genre,
open the door and say, "this is the way."

Dreams don't tell stories.
Nothing but a plan,
the pre-workings
to find the best way out.

Dreams dry up.
They crumble through fingertips
when growth never shows,
when the fire fades.

Dreams are fake.
Crying alone in thin air,
then the rain falls
and washes away all the proof.

A dream is a dream, if you don't walk all over it.

Shine Your Guns

The solution to the pollution is fabricated complication,
in an easy world.
Shower yourself in problems while you swim in passive-aggressive outcomes,
in this easy world.
Die Hard was a movie, but if your guns are all ya got, then . . .
ya might as well build up the wall between us,
and this easy world.
Overpower the coward that shies from the fight when the peace is in the pie,
neglect the reflections that shine
in this valley-bottom creek that is
the easy world we live in.

No One Needs to Know!

He never took a picture of what he had seen.
No postcards, no letters to his mom.
Blues and sunlight's gleam will never prove where the kid has been.
Lies, exaggerations,
the story of his generation.
Worn-out boots the only proof
of any kind of existence.
Mattress stains, yellow grains of sand from only he could tell you where.

He runs on living through,
    "No one is interested in something you didn't do."
And no Post-it Notes on the internet will make him feel better
about that
so he'll try to live forever.
Maybe give his head for a bucket of lead.
    But only a fool would want that.
He could get addicted to booze and love,
give it all up at a young age.
    But only a rock star would do that.
So instead, he writes his story on the back side of his receipts and reads them to his dog,
    the only mind he could possibly bestow it to now.
His dog has since run away.
Now he sits,
guaranteed life is but a fleeting dream,
    no controller of the complex machine,
    no holder of the horrors,
    no hand of the dashing queen.

And with that said,
his blood and sex are as good as dead.
No more feeding the fire of approval.
Not even enough to drive another story told.
Instead, he holds close his gross tales, his receipts, and Post-it Notes
> The bare-breasted blondes he dopes in are gone.
>
> The peak-pounding parties.
>
> The self-sounding safaris.
>
> The aims of the arousing army

are now only a myth.
> There's no fucking "on the road,"
>
> no kiss-and-telling fairy tales,
>
> no bliss in expelling the details.

There is only one side to the chronicle now.
It's a crumpled-up list
of the things he's bought.

The First Sight Of William Wallace

Who were those mind terrorists that ate my brain in a
child's meditation?
A nightmare still haunting, still still,
still beyond belief.
Single, solo, and six.
>War in my room.

Rape and pillage in my teepee.
I'm not quite asleep and they are awake with me.
I'm not dead but they battle my visions as death breathes,
>behind drawn grey sheets.

Catapults of fire behind dark eyelids
>mean mugs striped blue,
>
>heavy-set breasts,
>
>arms strong,
>
>staring at me.

Wilted and worn,
my sweat drips as the blood shimmers in the mud,
my meditational catastrophe of six years old.

Sandpaper My Soul

Sandpaper my soul,
and let the glaciers go.
Erode every bit of me,
and let the glaciers grow.

Rough is the stuff I live for, so the ice and bees shouldn't have to.
Let them free
and take me, silently.
No one has to know.
Just let them go.
Sandpaper my soul.
Let my heart burn to coal.
Keep me locked up forever.
But let the birds and the bees go.

Erase my mind, take everything I own.
Just let the glaciers be,
forever known.

STUNT

Eight billion and climbing.
One hundred thousand feet and rising.
One thousand, two hundred and eighty one pages in the Bible and
there is always a second coming,
very soon,
to a town near you.
We'll watch it all go down on 4K high-definition TVs,
while virtually created women ride robot pee-pees.
Electric cars on Mars, why not?
The world lives within an alien apple that never rots. . . . So,
why not?

      I'm lost in this electric wasteland.

      I'm lost in this never-before-seen footage.

      I'm stuck in this never-ending stunt.

      I'm stuck amongst gross growth with no hopes in stunting it.

Growth that blows my simple wiring into
      shutting-down mode.
Expansion is avalanching small huts to mansions as the icebergs canter.
I'm frantic to slow down with no way to keep up.
No way to shake my rust as I fuss and cuss the name
      Elon Musk.
It must be really hard trying to save the world, but
you're freaking me the fuck out.
Where are you taking us?
I may trust if you say we must but hiding sounds more robust—
ya know, like "hush hush,
the robots we've created are hunting us."
I'm making fun but this real-life sci-fi movie isn't so funny to me!

What happen to horse-drawn carriages and life-long marriages, with eight kids?
Where are all the pay phones and love letters?
It's all hate mail and trendsetters,
Apps, taps, big-man tax, and contracts.
And one day it will all crash
and I'll be a little passive-aggressive about it,
but for now,

>I'm lost in this electric wasteland.
>I'm lost in the never-before-seen footage.
>I'm stuck in this never-ending stunt.
>I'm stuck amongst gross growth with no hopes of stunting it.

Ease Your Mind, My Sister

My mind is like a sieve.
The things I've learned, things I did.
Down through the floorboards and right out the front door.
Absorbed by the cold core of the old man on the front porch.

>So I ask you, my sister,
>Don't ask me the smart way out of this.
>That'll always be a mystery

for you, me, and the old man
to figure out.

The Storytellers

Three black crows playing tricks on each other,
stealing bread and drink from one another,
stealing secrets of the night like falling wing feathers.
Smarter than the average bear and bird, these fellars.
Storytellers, too,
masked liars who are surviving on the 3 a.m. night.
Watch them, if you dare,
listen, if you enjoy the screams.
Attention is for the taking.
Wild act in the making.
Eyes wide, you can't fake it
during Storyteller's Hour.

The crows, the cowards,
> the humans and all the beings, perhaps
> the tellers themselves in novels,
> the aware in worldly solutions and salutations,

all living to tell their stories.

Flooring or boring, it's bound to catch an ear,
and that's all anyone cares.
Opinions blurted and heard,
a kiss to the wrist, honey for the ego,
and a fist bump for respect.
Whether it's to a tee or make-believe,
whether you read it or scream it,
crow kaaww or cry wolf,
have living proof

with the scars to show.
Or you have your lips tightly sewn.

> We are all a single grain of sand,
> and everyone has their tail in their hand,
> for all to see.

> And look at me,

being rude,

> still chasing my tail.

BLOOD

I rely now on nature,
since nurture fell through.
I depend on my dreams,
since you left me hanging.
Would you meet me halfway
and pretend to accept
what is undone in your eyes?

> What will surpass time
> and carry on,
> if not blood?

Your age does not sit
quite right with your cries.
This world passes on
what is already gone.
Since when do old ways
shine light on new states
without expectations?

> What will surpass time
> and carry on,
> if not blood?

It's this time, in this place,
where egos fall, over our face.
Blind to the times
and your life, without mine.
A sneak peek at what stands

of my mind in your hands.
The great relief to not repeat
what was seen behind me.

Because we breathe
the same shit!
And we reap
the culprit.
It's seeing kin
with cold eyes.
It's missing out
on fresh skin!
It's the old man.
It's the young kid.
It's two ways
of judgement.
With one shot
at mistakes,
there's no guilt.
It's what we've raised.

>And what will surpass time
>and carry on
>if not

blood?

I Can't Call It

Trump wears a different suit,
call it number five.
She wears a high-heeled boot,
lives in limbo's fire.
These fools fool for distraction
not to hurt the heart.
Fools fool for satisfaction
to keep the joke alive.
Wipe that shit off your shoulder
or let it rip your white flag flesh.
Lay your hands clean of diamonds,
shake off your laceless shoes.
Find yourself in the limelight,
tighten your loosest screws.
Shine your halogen spotlight
and now who's fooling who.

> There's no way to say it's wrong
> unless you've tasted its death.
> There's no way to sing out of tune
> unless you've sung before.

There is no possible answer
when everything is being questioned.
Read the writings, write what you've heard.
Don't be shy when it all disappears.
The brilliant will blunder
from a swollen mind.

All that is cool and lordly
will crack with the trends.
The suffering will subside
when the blind can see the blue.
Power will be thrown aside
to suck autumn's afternoon dew.
The submissive will stand
with a rise from the minority.
The angry will bow
when the poor need no more.

> There's no way to say it's wrong
> unless you've tasted its death.
> There's no way to sing out of tune
> unless you've danced before.

Popularity is a bust
and sitting alone is sinful.
Religion is ignorant
And doubt is irrelevant.
There is dread in a fight
but closing your eyes is giving it all up.
A revolution is demanding
and erases all hope of the past.
Progression is greedy
and being satisfied is lackadaisical.
There is change in all of us
but tradition has gotten us here.

Sticking to your guns can be powerful
when those at peace back down
and opinions matter...
But that's not for me to say.

> There's no way to say it's wrong,
> unless you've tasted its death.
> There's no way to sing out of tune,
> unless you've created the song.

This One's for Them

I stand beside those who have been wronged, ridden, riddled, bitten, drugged, used, abused, fused, directed, infected, ill-protected; who've been disconnected from self by some sort of fucked-up system horny for control. This is in full support of those who have been mind-fucked, physically tucked and socially swept away by a more powerful hand. And I scream this from the raspiest parts of my whiskey-coated throat for those who are unable to voice themselves properly.

This one is for every lip-smacking preacher who pushes to form young minds into moulds like they are Jesus, every dream-flopping pest who thinks they are superior, every single simple my-way-or-the-highway Soviet, every horse blinded booty-shaker forcefully breeding celebrities, every powerful parent feeding fixed pictures of the future, every comma-using capitalist with a boner to say "you can't write like that," every entitled shamer shattering the gift of an immortal's mind.
For the rule-makers.
The gay haters.
The fucking trend-setters and the ones putting price tags on beauty.
This is for the advertisers, salesmen, shitty lawyers and the bulls that set this brainwashing path.
This one is for the corporation.
The Man!
The Man with the hammer.
The Woman with the mallet.
The nun with the ruler stick.
This one is for every white bathroom there ever was and to the *fuck* that told someone to go put those five letters on the door, W-H-I-T-E.
This one is for every link of chain hand-made for a brother.

It's for every border guard officer with a life-taker in his holster.
Every prime minister piercing through feathers and fur with arms locked and loaded while our arms raise and our songs pray for the land to stay untainted.
It's for every American-made demand for shit-starting the world has ever seen.
It's for the dice that will be rolled next to decide the future of war.
It's for every bullet fired in preparation.
It's for the fingers on triggers and for the young minds dutifully following.
And this one is for the medications that may have caused that.
The occupations that strive to create a norm.
It's for the dedication directed to building walls and forms.
It's for the news that gets casted to persuade weak eyes.
This one goes out to those who whisper disease in the ears of the pleading.

Fuck you!

Old Friend

Is this a rebirth or is this what being sober feels like?
Are you watching now, Dad?
You impressed yet?
Would you call me a man yet?
Well, either way,
I'm not drinking right now
and I'm working hard on everything else.
How 'bout you?
Still drinking?
You happy yet?
Or has your definition of happy just always been beyond my eyes?
Eh, by the way,
> when are you coming home?
> And why don't you ask me that?

Yeah, I moved away,
but you left me, man,
just when I was becoming interesting.
Interesting.
You proud of me yet, Dad?
Well, I'll be straight with you,
I'm twenty-two and don't own much.
I don't have any money saved.
I might be an alcoholic
and I'm definitely not working all year-round.
So how 'bout it?
You proud of me yet?
I know none of this seems very impressive, but
if by some freak chance I could impress you,

would you just be my friend?
Would you sit around a campfire and drink whiskey out of the bottle with me?
Would you stick your thumb out to come see me?
Would you bail me out of jail?
Fuck, would you just sit down and listen to "Blunderbuss" with me and get excited about something we both love?
Would you do all this 'cause we're friends and I asked you to
or would that be pushing it!?
No pressure or anything,
but I figured if you were willing to go through fifteen years of dealing with me ya might as well stick around and try to enjoy the aftermath.
'Cause there is a chance that my "boy to man" verse and your, "man to old man sitting all alone in his home" curse might just mesh
if we sat down and talked about women and love for once.
You could stand up and let your hopes for me come out bluntly and I could tell you how,

> "I know I'm not your success story but I am turning pages, Dad, losing them, making them up and sometimes swallowing them whole. All the wealth in this story I consume is mine and you won't understand. We could trade an eye for an eye and try to see each other, but, Dad, let's just be friends and pretend like we are two different people for once."

This period of us being men together couldn't be any more vital in getting to know each other again.
I want to know about your adulting problems and you can show me how to be a man

I want to tell you about growing up in this new generation and I can try to show you how to enjoy it.

But I know:

I bet a brand new house,

five cars, two dogs,

a successful business, and one rich women can take up a lot of a man's time. So . . .

only time and our love will tell. But till then,

I guess I'll see ya when I see ya,

old friend.

The Ballad of Johnny Peterson

    His stoned fingertips move smooth like glass.
    Mastered is every intricate delivery,
    hidden and humble.
It all breeds through twine wrapped around two pegs,
    the sound of being electrified
    by poetry
Without a word.
    Nothing new, he's a magician.
I meant musician but, hey,
    you'll never read his name and that's the way it should be.
The public swell of his art will hide behind our beatnik walls of this
degenerated-by-our-generation generation.
The "2000 and somethings."

He's the dime in the dozen—no dime a dozen and he's ten cents short
of a dime sometimes. He lost a thousand dimes last night.
    Along with his shame, thank fuck!
And, oh, does he fuck!
    With balls on couch cushion, dick straight in party's mouth and
    blondes, too,
    for all to see and dream. Erect,
    we were, our white dresses floating in the steam of some apart-
    ment atop a tattoo parlour in the pissy city streets.
Oh, is he the halo in the devil's night!
And blasphemy to my sideways heart that beats for the blondes!
    Long, curly haired knight,
    riding bodacious purebreds thru realms with a spotlight.
    The drive is unknown.

His family life is unknown, but
he says "I love you" to me, not his father.
But thank the Mother of good reason for whoever raised his careless ass
'cause his youth will not fade.

> He carries his toothbrush and his wallet along with week-old
> beer caps all in the same front pocket of his four-year-old red
> shorts that have outlasted my will to stick my thumb out.
> His sorry looking rucksack will never die along with his dental
> floss stitches that exist in all the clothes he owns except his
> under-britches, which are completely non-existent because his
> willy is free like the peach fuzz on his upper lip that screams:

"I don't give a fuck!"

He has home bum status,

> trading the dirty shirt off his back in the bum's business bushes
> with sweet, sweet malt liquor flowing down his bear chest, as he
> hops a railcar headed for mardi gras or shambala or some hippy
> hoedown where love is dipped in baking sugars and devoured
> like Dunkaroos and dirty boxed red wine chases it all down.

And the way he puffs only half a cigarette after all this shows his

> Penny-pinching, clinching stinky ciggy, butt-
> smoker ways,
>
> the ways of a saint and brilliant, I say.

He writes a record-breaking sci-fi thriller on the back of his hand while
he kills hitchhiking feats in bare feet, and breaking the laws cause he's
too pretty.
In desert sands he sleeps while receiving dirty gypsy tattoos from naked
women claiming him a year-round home in the slabs themselves,

> Codeine dreams while someone's girlfriend screams,

"I need you!"

He puts her to sleep with the words of some god he has read
about, and gives her a name the wind speaks.

With an owl perched on his forearm he protects her from the
night that is filled with a crazy tea she has never tried before.

She fades away in his teepee beneath the mother moon that he milked
of any disease before leaving her side for good.

And I saw him fall in love ONCE!

    Chubby cheeked, beautiful heap of bones she was

    that straightened him up with organics but folded his spine with

    a dirty habit,

    drink,

    as she headed north.

I drank with him 'cause we are both really good at that now
and whiskey also sews with dental-floss stitches,

    thank gosh.

Between a trip home and sips of any bottle,

    his heart was mended

    and driven back into the dirt,

        with the trees.

But only he really knows the whole truth.
And most of it is written in hidden forbidden journals you'll never read.
This, is just
what I have seen.

I would like to thoroughly thank everyone who was around at all for the writing of this book/ these poems. There would be no story, no love, no listeners, nothing to write about without all the people I am overly grateful to call my family and friends—so, thank you. In particular, I would like to mention Preston Gray, Keelan Horne, Drew Bryan, Georgia Jones, Gillian Ellis, Jack, my wonderful sister, my dad and dearest of all, my mother. You have been there through it all and I will forever be indebted to each and every one of you. Thanks. Love.

Printed in Canada